Values-Based
Diversity
Generational Change At
Work

Jody Holland

OPENING QUOTE

The idea of stereotyping is an idea of limiting the potential of a person. It isn't about building their success. It is about building a box to place them inside of. The strength of our workforce lies in embracing our differences! This begins with understanding, moves into acceptance, and finishes with embracing differences.

The values that each of us has are a result of the way that we labeled our experiences throughout life. In each of the three stages of psychological development, we create a little more of our self-definition. We are who we are simply as a result of the way that we define our world. It is in the understanding of who a person is, based on their perceptions, that we are able to connect at a deeper level, attain greater work performance, and inspire greatness in others.

CONTENTS

ACKNOWLEDGMENTS

I would like to acknowledge all of the leaders throughout the years that have shown me what works and what doesn't work in business. I have learned from the good, the bad, and the ugly. I am thankful for all of those experiences.

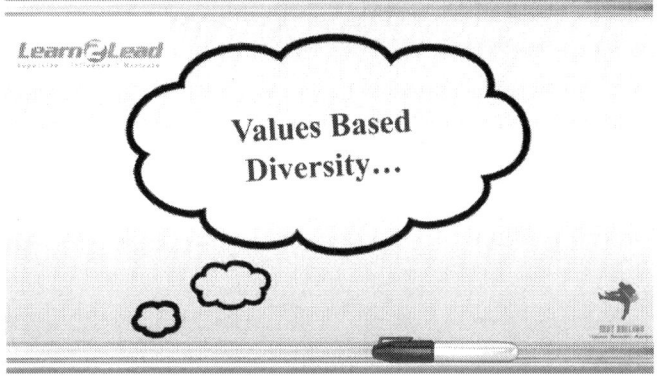

Learning Objectives

Identify four generations in the workplace, and define them by experiences and events.

Compare and contrast the values and the potential outcomes of generational interaction.

Consider and identify potential problems for an organization when people from different generations fail to communicate effectively.

Compare and identify differing feedback styles and their impact.

Offer strategies for effective cross generational communication, supervision and direction.

5

Mixing & Matching 4 Generations At Work

Gen-Z	Millennials	Generation Xers	Baby Boomers	Traditionalists
0% of the workforce	40% of the workforce	35% of the workforce	24% of the workforce	1% of the workforce

Why Do We Have Conflict

Many organizations experience generational conflict. Older leaders have a hard time understanding, and therefore trusting, younger ones who are anxious to find their role in leadership. The latter often can't understand why older leaders believe and do what they do, and their questioning may lead to conflict.

Generational Tensions

Most of this tension results from generational differences that exist because of contrasting values. We make choices and decisions based on our value system, and differing values often lead to misunderstandings and misinterpretation. This, in turn, hampers our relationships and lessens the effectiveness of our work together.

Why Learn About Generations?

✓ Changing Demographics

✓ Better Understanding of How To Connect

✓ Better Communication

✓ Better Teamwork & Leadership

Who You Are When...

It's not just what you do that matters. It is who you are while you are interacting with others that matters.

You Are Your Thoughts

The events and conditions that happened during our formative years helped to shape the world-view that we adopted.

Because of the labels that we place on those events and experiences, we end up seeing the world through that filtered lens.

Stages To Being You

Dr. Morris Massey
stated that there are 3
stages of development
that each of us goes
through to become
who we are.

Imprinting – Stage 1

Up To Your 7th
Birthday…

Your brain operates
differently.

You develop
personality.

Modeling – Stage 2

From 7 to our 14th Birthday…

We develop values and beliefs

We model others.

Socialization – Stage 3

From 14 to 22ish…

We test our values.

We learn critical thinking, decision-making, and accountability.

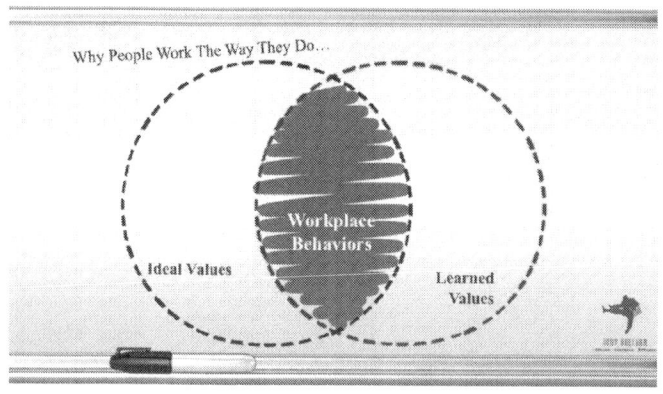

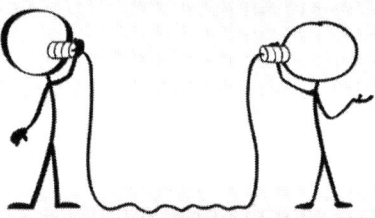

Traditionalists

- Born between 1922 and 1945
- Experienced the Great Depression
- and World War II
- Valued financial security, teamwork, sacrifice, delayed gratification, and the government which got them through these ordeals
- Their values more closely resembled biblical values; extended families were close, and marriages lasted a lifetime

Baby Boomers

- Born from 1946-1964
- Arrived to postwar affluence and the indulgence of parents who wanted them to have a better life than theirs
- More aware of political and social issues and became more and more disillusioned with government, big business, traditional religion, and parents
- Values included self-fulfillment, individualism, and material wealth
- 80 Million People

Generation Xers

- Born between 1965 and 1980
- The 1st Generation To Enter The Workforce after Corporate Downsizing
- Grew up independent
- They work hard and play hard and define themselves by things outside of work.
- 46 Million People

Millennials

- Born between 1981 and 2000
- Much more positive relationships with parents
- More often rewarded for participating than previous generations
- Incredible at juggling information
- 75 Million People

Generation Z

- Born between 2001 and 2020 (estimated)
- More protected than previous generations
- Lived with significantly more structure than previous generations
- Started working in 2016 (first wave)
- Estimated 76 Million People

Generational Experiences

- Experience influences behavior
- It doesn't determine behavior
- Everyone has free will
- Ultimately, it is the label that we create for the event, not the event itself that matters.

Events & Experiences

Traditionalists:
- Great Depression
- New Deal
- World War II
- Korean War

Boomers:
- Civil Rights
- Sexual Revolution
- Cold War
- Space travel
- Assassinations

Events & Experiences

GenXers:
- Fall of Berlin Wall
- Watergate
- Women's Liberation
- Desert Storm
- Energy Crisis

Millennials:
- School shootings
- Oklahoma City
- Technology
- Child focused world
- Clinton / Lewinsky

Generational Values

Traditionalists:
- Hard work
- Dedication & sacrifice
- Respect for rules
- Duty before pleasure
- Honor

Baby Boomers:
- Optimism
- Team orientation
- Personal gratification
- Involvement
- Personal growth

Generational Values

Xers:
- Diversity
- Techno literacy
- Fun and informality
- Self-reliance
- Pragmatism

Millennials:
•Optimistic
•Feel civic duty
•Confident
•Achievement oriented
•Respect for diversity

What Generations Want

Traditionalists:

- Try New Things
- Be respected for experience
- Be respected for loyalty

Baby Boomers:

·Recognition without reminders

·Be respected for their contribution

·Be rewarded for their success

Generational Values

Generation Xers:

- Work independently
- Be respected for results
- Be able to leave when the work is done
- Be relaxed

Millennials:

- Work as a team
- Be trusted to get the job done
- Be trained in the job and other skills
- Be very casual

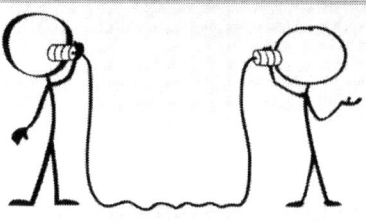

Making Sure We Are Clear...

Each person gets to shape and reshape themselves throughout their lives. You are responsible for you!

Every employee should be held to the same standard. No adaptation should be made that compromises the integrity of the job or diminishes the effectiveness of your department to carry out its mission. All employees should comply with policies and procedures set forth by their department and company.

VALUES IN...	TRADITIONALISTS	BOOMERS	GENXERS	MILLENNIALS
MOTHER	Homemaker	Working Mother	Single Mother	Single Mother/ Father
FAMILY	Close Family	Dispersed Family	Latchkey Kids	Looser Family Structure
MARRIAGE	Married Once	Divorced / Remarried	Single Parent	Undetermined
HAIR	Short Hair	Long Hair	Any Style Hair	Bleached/ Spiked
CLOTHES	Formal	Casual	Bizarre	Anything Goes
MUSIC	Big Band/ Swing	Rock 'n' Roll	Alternative, Rap	Very Diverse
MONEY	Save It Now	Buy It Now	Want It Now	Get It Now (online)
PURCHASING	Purchase w/ Cash	Purchase w/ credit card	Struggling to Purchase	Purchase Online
MARKETING	Ford Marketing Concept	GE Marketing Concept	Ignored Market	Interactive Global Market
HIGH-TECH	Slide Rule	Calculator	Computer	Internet
WORK STYLE	Team Work	Personal Fulfillment	Tentative/ Divided Loyalty	Networking
WAR	Win a War	Why a War?	Watch A War	Winless War
MORALS	Puritan Ethics	Sensual	Cautious	Tolerant

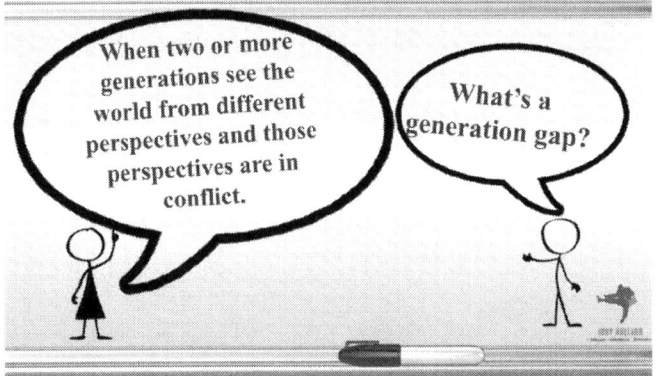

Estimated Workforce By The End Of 2017

Traditionalists – 0% of the national workforce

Baby Boomers – 18% of the national workforce

Generation X – 39% of the national workforce

Generation Y – 43% of the national workforce

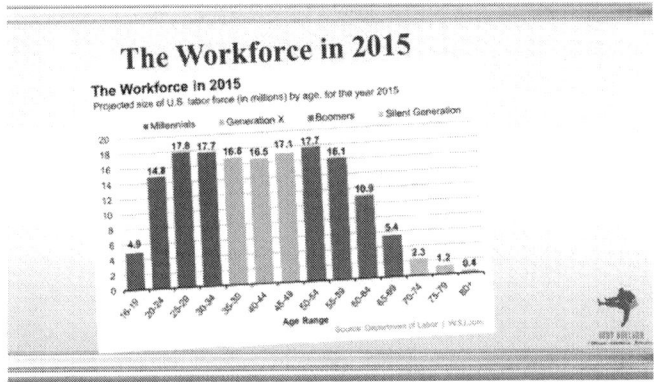

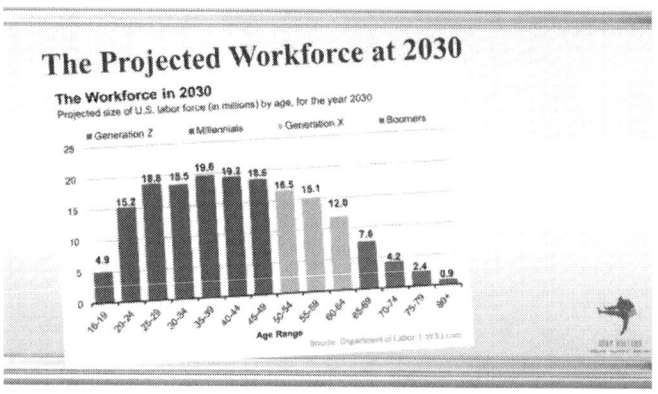

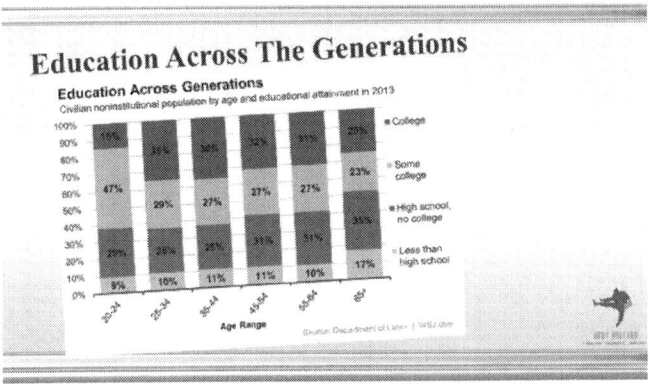

A Half Century of Change

1956

- Domestic Economy
- Working 9 to 5 with holidays off
- Formal / Professional Dress
- Work at the "office"
- Corporate Ladder

2006

- Global Economy
- Working 24/7 – 365
- Casual / Trendy Dress
- Work at the "coffee" or anywhere
- Corporate Labyrinth

These demographic changes will have profound impacts on organizations.

Human resource management will become a critical success factor as companies have to focus on:

- Recruitment
- Retention of employees of all ages
- Succession planning
- Work-life balance
- Career Development

What Does This Mean To You?

The world of work as it was in 2000 will not exist again.

--Recruiting is different

--Managing is different

--Diversity is different

Managing Generational Diversity

Old Model	New Model
•Loyalty to institution	• Free agency
•Rank, hierarchy and following rules	• Autonomy and independence
•System and process	• Action and results
•Safety, security, don't rock the boat	• Challenge, risk and innovation
•Career and advancement	• Work-life balance

41

How Do You Attract New Talent Now?

- Minimize barriers to entering the workforce
- Have consistent training & development
- Create a fun atmosphere
- Do things that build relationships between your workers… outside of work

Values Based Diversity

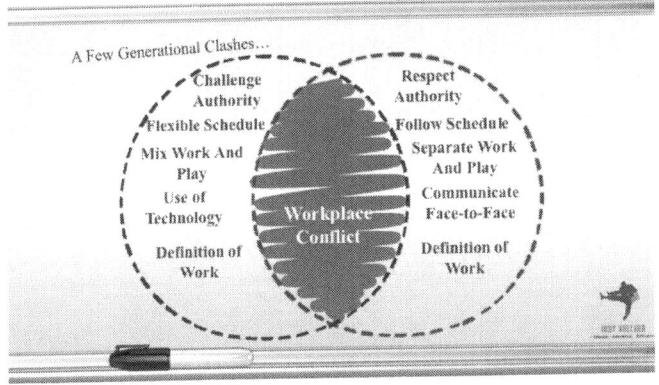

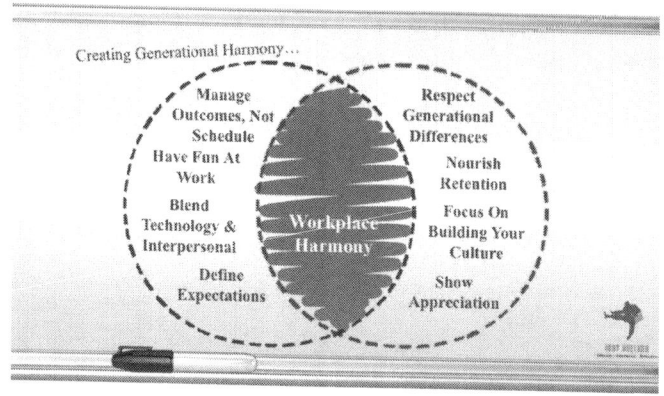

Values Based Diversity

Communication Expectations

Traditionalists   Boomers   Gen Xers   Millenials

No news is good news!   Feedback once a year with documentation   How did I do on this project?   How did I do today?

Feedback Styles Differ

Feedback styles that may appear informative and helpful to one generation might seem formal and "preachy" to another.

Feedback a GenXer thinks is immediate and honest can seem hasty or even inappropriate to other generations.

Some older generations have been told that there is a time and place for feedback. Younger generations haven't necessarily been taught this "rule."

Feedback Styles Differ

Traditionalists seek no applause but appreciate a subtle acknowledgement that they have made a difference.

Boomers are often giving feedback to others but seldom receiving, especially positive feedback.
Xers need positive feedback to let them know they're on the right track.

Millennials are used to praise and may mistake silence for disapproval. They need to know what they're doing right and what they're doing wrong.

Resolving Differences

✓ Give every generation a voice

✓ Invest in the success of all of your people

✓ Build relationships

Create Understanding

Understanding other points of view and allowing for differences helps people communicate and get along.

Don't jump to conclusions on others until you understand their perspective.

Accept People Where They Are

Acceptance is crucial to every relationship, and a basic need for healthy self-esteem.

Acceptance of someone doesn't mean we have to approve of what he/she believes or does.

We can accept someone as having worth, even if we can't always agree.

Sometimes acceptance involves trust and even some risk.

Forgive & Choose Your Labels

People often hold on to grudges and prejudices far longer than they should.

If someone from another generation has "wronged" you, understand that it was one person

You get to decide what meaning you assign to things in your life, and ONLY you!

Embracing Diversity

Each of us has our own unique characteristics. But, it is our differences that make our lives together interesting and rewarding.

Everyone has something to contribute. We all need to remember to accept others for who they are and look for the best that they have to offer. That is what valuing diversity is all about!

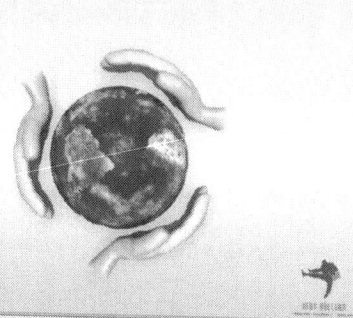

Thank You For Your Attention
THANK you!

2 BOOK SUMMARY

It is not just what you do that matters. It is who you are while you are doing it.

We are ultimately the sum total of the values that guide us in life. We treat people the way that we do because of the values that we have. We listen to the music that we do because it reflects our values. We associate with certain people because they compliment our values or they represent the values that we "think" that we would like to express.

The debate has been around for quite some time as to whether we are born with our values or we they develop. Do our values come from some genetic encoding or are they blended from genetics and from environment. Or, are we simply a "product of our raising?" The question that each of us has to answer is...

Why am I who I am?

Dr. Morris Massey, sociologist and great thinker of developmental thoughts, outlined the process of you becoming you into three distinct stages. The age bracket for these stages can vary, based on the development of the individual as well as the times in which they grew up. However, there are three specific stages that seem to guide us into becoming the people that we are today. These stages are...

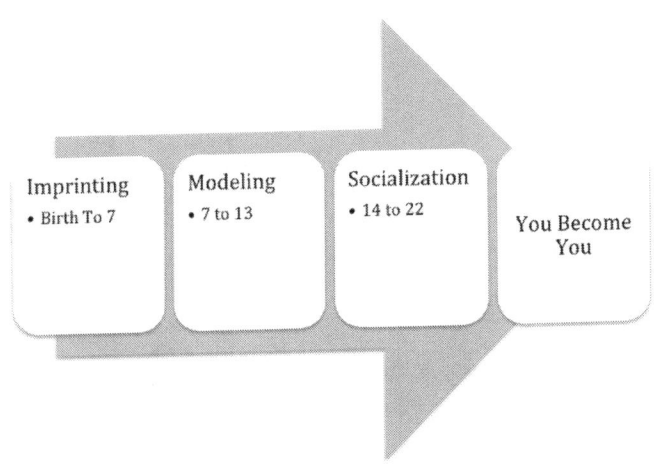

Imprinting
• Birth To 7

Modeling
• 7 to 13

Socialization
• 14 to 22

You Become You

Imprinting

During this stage, we simply soak things up like a sponge. We are constantly observing what is going on around us, what our parents or guardians are teaching us, how they are behaving, and what right and wrong are. Most of us heard the word, "NO" as much as we heard any other word during this stage. Because we soak things up and accept them, generally, as truth, we can often create false beliefs in our own minds. We are looking to our parents, primarily, as the bearers and creators of truth. This means that, if they have a false truth as their belief, we are likely to adopt the same belief. Right and wrong, good and bad, according to Massey, are human constructs. We often assume that they would exist even without us, but they are a definition that we have established in our minds.

Think about the idea of exposing two children to completely different environments. One is brought up with kindness and sharing and compassion. The other is brought up with anger and hatred. These two environment will be what they child knows as the truth of their lives. It is during the second stage of development that a child will begin to find someone else to model, outside of their parents or guardians. This first stage is critical for establishing the underlying characteristics of their personality makeup.

According to Christopher Nave, from the University of California, at Riverside, our personality is almost completely set by the end of first grade. His study observed children at the age of 7 and tracked their behaviors into early adulthood. Personality and behavioral indicators that were present in first grade, remained present in the subjects' adult lives. This means that during the first stage of development, as defined by Massey, we are developing strong behavioral and personality pathways. These will very likely stick with us for the rest of our lives.

It is important to create the best environment possible for young people, which includes chores and responsibilities. As a young person, when you learn at this early stage to be responsible for your actions and to be responsible for accomplishing work, then you are likely to carry that behavior pattern with you as an adult.

It is this author's theory that many young people today rely on their parents for financial support because they were not conditioned to be responsible at this early stage. Had parents held their kids accountable made them be responsible for chores, sticking with tasks, and taking care of themselves, as was done in the older generations, the work ethic and reliability of that child as an adult would be different.

Modeling

If you want to know how a person sees the world, discover their heroes. When you can identify the people that they look up to, you will see what the value and belief systems of the person are. You will see what they desire to model as the right path for themselves. This modeling takes place as children, between the ages of 7 and 13, look around their world and choose who they want to emulate. They may choose teachers, religious leaders, sports figures, family, or even comic book heroes. Whoever they decide to look up to will have a strong impact on what they decide is the right path for their life.

Think back to when you were in 4th or 5th grade. Who was it that you looked up to? Was it your parents, your friends, the cool kid at school, or someone else? Take just a minute and write down who your hero was at that age and what was it about them that made you want to be like them.

My hero was: _____

This was my hero because: _____

_____

_____

_____

The age of 10 is the most critical age in a young person's life in regards to the development of values, according to Massey. This is generally about 4th or 5th grade. It is when a young person chooses the most critical values and beliefs in their lives. They will develop their construct of integrity, relationship, work ethic, reliability, and a host of others during this time. Think about the difference in experiences that each of the generations had. Think about what your grandparents' life was like versus what your parents' life versus your own. How old were you when you began working? How old were you when you because responsible for taking care of yourself? How old were you when you began to truly be held accountable for your choices?

When I was 23 years old, I was attending a professional development course in the Dallas-Ft. Worth area. The speaker at this program looked out at the group of Generation Xers, me included, and said…

What really scares me is that I am looking at a group of people who never had heroes. You never had anyone that you looked up to.

I have never really been the type of person to hold my tongue, so I raised my hand to respond to what he had said. He pointed to me and I said the following…

That's not true. I had plenty of heroes when I was growing up. I looked up to Batman and Robin, Superman, Spiderman, The Green Lantern, Captain America, and even the Wonder-Twins.

He shook his head side to side and let out an audible sigh. *Those are not real people!*

I let a half grin go across my face and said, *Oh, well what about the Incredible Hulk? I met him when I was 12. That dude is huge!*
Side note: It turns out that was just Lou Ferigno painted green, but it was still very impressive to me.

He went on to chastise us for not looking up to political heroes and war heroes. The reality was that politics had been exposed as corrupt to us. We had seen so much of the darkness that existed in that realm that had not been brought to light for his generation. The difference in the heroes made a difference in what I valued and found important in my own life. It does for each and every one of us. Think about the heroes that you described in this chapter and what the characteristics, values, and behaviors of that hero were, or are. How many of those do you strive to emulate? We created our ideal version of ourselves as young people and often strive to live into that self as we get older.

Socialization

The socialization period is from the ages of 14 to roughly 22 years old. This is a time of questioning what we have been taught is right and wrong. It is a time of challenging the construct of reality and values that our parents or guardians gave us. It is a time that people often experiment with which belief system will define them for the rest of their lives.

During this time, we are largely influenced by our peers. We are watching what they do, how they think, what they believe, and how they behave. We are often seeking to get our cues on what we should be doing from them. Thinking back on my own life, I know that it was very important which people I chose to associate with. There were times that I was friends with the "wrong people" and I ended up in trouble and heading down a path that lead to problems later in life. There were also times that I was connected with people that brought out the best in me, challenged me, and pushed me to be more, do more, and have more than I would have otherwise.

We are also influenced by the multimedia input that we absorb. We are watching for what people should b be like in the shows, movies, and even in the games that we play. Young people will often attempt to take on the persona of the characters that they look up to. If our teenagers are being continuously exposed to characters that are deviant, it changes their perspective on what the right behavior set is or should be for them. From my own experience, when I watched shows with violence in them as a teenager, I became more comfortable with the idea of violence. When I was watching fighting programs regularly, I began fighting more myself. This is not to say that if a person watches James Bond they will become a spy for Her Majesty's Secret Service. It is meant to simply point out that we are continuously persuaded and influenced by the things that we expose ourselves to. Within the lives of my kids, when they watch shows where the kids are disrespectful to their parents, I see a marked difference in the way that they communicate with my wife and me.

When I was a teenager, the show "Beverly Hills 90210" was very popular. In this show, the kids were basically on their own to do whatever they wanted to do. The parents were there, but they barely registered as influencers in their lives. They were rich, had great cars, and could party whenever they wanted to. Those values were like the holy grail of teenage-dom. They resonated with the generation of young people as the ideal setup and therefore people were attracted to the show. Think about the shows that you were attracted to as a young person. What were the values of the characters and the overall theme of the show? Did those values represent the "ideal" setup for you?

The saying that many of our mothers used on us when we were in this stage was, "Be careful who you hang out with. You will end up just like them." This was the harsh truth that is still relevant today. Even beyond this developmental stage, it is our associations that help to create us. Massey simply understood that this was a sociological principle of development.

The Generations At Work

There are four distinctive generations at work today, with a 5th one on the way. Each of the generations has a unique perspective on reality, as defined through their experiences. The three stages of psychological development, that you just reviewed, each held a different set of experiences for the generations. Think about what you experienced, for example, in 5th grade. What was school like? What did you do during your summer break from school? Now, think about what a 5th grader today would experience. Some of the differences between today's 5th grader and what you were like as a 5th grader actually hold the key to why people work differently from one another.

Let's travel back in time to 1932, to the Traditionalist generation. This generation was born from 1922-1945. Imagine that you are in 5th grade, assuming you are in school at all. Summer break comes around and it is time to be off from school for the next 90 or so days. Just like last year, you go to work for your family. You just don't work for money from your parents. Instead, working for your parents is simply an expectation for being a part of the family. You get up at 5AM every day in order to take care of the animals. At 5:15, you head out the door with a biscuit that your mom made that morning from scratch. She was up at 4:15 to get breakfast ready for the family. You work until 11:30 that morning and then stop work in the field. You head toward the one shade tree that exists at the edge of the field. In a few minutes, your mom shows up with lunch for everyone. You drink some lemonade and eat your sandwich as you rest a little from the hard work. At around 12:15 PM, you go back to work and you work until 6PM that evening. Your family, like many families during that time of depression, works hard for everything that they have. You don't waste anything. You don't walk away from your food because it isn't the brand name, microwave meal, that you really wanted. You eat what you have, and it is often what you grew or raised, not what you bought. You see only your family during the week. Church was often the only time that you saw anyone besides family or a close neighbor during the summertime. You didn't have a TV to watch and you only listened to the radio on Saturday night for the weekly show. You entertained yourself when you weren't working, which wasn't often. You didn't have extra money. Not many people had extra money.

During this time in the United States, only 9% of women worked outside of the home. Unemployment hit as high as 35%. This meant that 35% of able-bodied people who wanted to find a job, couldn't find one. If you compound that with the gender roles, it means that more than 50% of our country was out of work. 61% of men were active duty military at one point or another during their lives. This one fact alone helps to explain the methodology of management that exists and existed as they entered into leadership roles. They believed in hierarchical structure, which meant that communication and leadership all flowed from one level to another, and that sticking around meant the opportunity for a promotion. Tenure meant success! Respect of authority was tantamount to having your next opportunity. Work was formal. Dress was formal. Structures were formal. Communication was formal. Everything at work was structured, just like their childhood seemed to be.

Now let's move forward a generation, to the Baby Boomer generation. 5th grade for the first of this generation was in 1956. The birth years for this generation were from 1946-1964. America was booming and "Leave it to Beaver" land was in full swing. Many young people did jobs like mowing, delivering newspapers, and chores for their parents and neighbors. With the economy booming and fewer people making their living on the farm, your summer looks quite a bit different. You have time to play sandlot baseball with your friends after your chores are done. Parental roles were beginning to change some, but moms were still seen as the one that takes care of the home. More moms were working outside of the home, but that was still minority. Your life was much more stable than your parents' or even your grandparents' lives. You saw the possibilities in life and believed that you could do anything that you put your mind to. You knew that you could be rich and successful if that is what you decided to do. You were the first generation in your family to plan on going to college and the first generation that would have the opportunity to break out of the socio-economic molds that previous generations of your family were in. You still worked hard, but you also played hard. Your family and your teachers have conditioned you that you are what you do for a living.

The next generation to enter the scene is the Generation Xers. This generation grew up in a time where technology was crashing onto the scene. They went from only being able to see local news to knowing what was going on in other countries. MTv made a splash by allowing people to see their favorite bands performing their songs. Cable boxes (12 whole channels at first) connected this group with the rest of the world and shortened the distance between geographical locations. From 1968 to 1972, the percentage of women in the paid labor force (their moms) went from 25% to 47%. During that same timeframe, the divorce rate rose from 25% to 45%. 1972 was the first year in US history for the divorce rate to be lower than the percentage of women in the paid labor force. As a result of the increase in working moms and the lack of "daycare" facilities, many of the young people from this generation simply went home to an empty house after school.

The term "latch-key" kids was created for this generation because they made it home with a key on a string around their necks for the latch. They grew up with a very broad freedom and independence because of the amount of alone time they had to themselves. This generation, born between 1965 and 1980, is the smallest of the generations in America. Their birth years cycle was shorter than other generations, as well as other social factors that reduced the number of births during these years. In total, there are 46 million people born into Generation X, which is 34 million fewer people than the baby boomer generation. Their values were things such as autonomy, freedom, independence, and time for themselves. They were the first generation NOT to define themselves by the work that they did.

Next comes the Millennial Generation. This generation is a very unique mix of parents. Some are Boomers married to Xers, Boomers remarried to Boomers, and Xers married to Xers. This generation grew up with a much more positive experience a friendlier relationship with their parents. Their parents were often their friends, which is different than the majority of previous generational experiences. Their sports involvement changed and the idea of teamwork over winning started floating to the surface. Interestingly enough, they were often rewarded for simply participating, yet their parents pushed them to excel in multiple activities simultaneously, including academics. Many of these young people grew up competing in two and three sports while striving to maintain status in the National Honor Society. This drive made them feel both pressured and driven, and yet many of them needed the safety-net of their parents' support and continuous recognition to keep going.

With 75 million people born into this generation between the years of 1980 and 2000, and the push of their parents to be in charge as quickly as possible, they jumped into work with an expectation that they would be recognized just like they were when they were competing as kids. This is likely the only way that they could have seen the world, since this is the way that they were conditioned to see the world. The very people that conditioned them to expect more for themselves than previous generations were often the loudest opponents to this type of thinking at work. Many parents of Millennial kids intended for only their own kid to be further ahead than the others. They were also very frustrated when other people's kids had that expectation. This generations, just like the others, is simply a product of how they were raised by parents, media, and society as a whole. They were taught to think the way that they think.

The final of the five current generations is being dubbed Generation Z. This generation is still being born as of 2016, they are estimated to be as large as the Millennial generation by 2020. Their birth years began in 2001. This generation has faced an even greater challenge than the Millennial generation did in the formation of their values. This challenge will most definitely impact their work as well as society. The challenge that they face is that of a lack of accountability. Just a few examples that were submitted in the research for this book include...

- A 6th grader's parents selling their house and moving to a new town in order to keep their kid from facing discipline for pulling a fire alarm
- A 5th grader's parents moving to a new part of the district to avoid her being

punished for bringing Vodka to school and sharing with other 5th graders.

- A 9th grader's parents threatening to sue the school district if they punished their daughter for stealing a test from a teacher and helping other students cheat.
- A 3rd grader's parents suing the school district because their child was made to sit in the corner after acting out in class.
- A 4th grader's parents launching a campaign to remove a principle for "giving excessive tardies" to their child when he was consistently late to school more than 10 times in 20 days.
- A 4th grader's parents lobbying to get a teacher fired for counting off on homework that was turned in obviously done in the Mother's handwriting.

Time and time again, this generation has been overprotected by their parents and have not learned the lesson of being accountable for their behaviors. In the name of keeping their kids safe, a generation of parents is raising a generation of kids who will be shocked when they are fired for not showing up to work, or for not doing their work. The challenge of creating a belief in accountability is a tough one and will require tremendous skill as a supervisor. Being able to modify beliefs is at the core of what a supervisor will have to do by 2021.

Notes

Values Based Diversity

Jody N Holland * www.JodyHolland.com

ABOUT THE AUTHOR

Jody Holland received his B.A. in Communications from Angelo State University in 1994. He has received specialized training and certifications in physiognomy, conversational hypnosis, team-building, leadership, management, and pre-hire testing. Jody's clients would say that his capacity for creating ROI is what they appreciate the most. He normally gets between a 10X and 25X return on their investment. He has been sought after by clients to speak at their retreats, to assist in changing behaviors in top executives as well as coaching C-Suite leaders for success. Jody has had the opportunity to train and do business in 14 countries and all across the United States. Jody has worked with clients ranging from regional companies to the Fortune 50, including companies like Walmart Corporate, Lockheed Martin, Boeing, and many more. He has worked with First Financial Bancshares, the Community Banker's Association of Illinois, the Illinois Funeral Director's Association, the Illinois State Chamber of Commerce, Leadership Texas, Workforce Development Boards, etc. Jody has been the keynote speaker more than 200 times at conferences and has trained more than 200,000 leaders on topics ranging from generational change at work, to sales, to service, to authentic communication and a variety of other topics focused on interpersonal interactions.

Jody is the author of 12 books, which can be found on Amazon.com, including books on leadership, time management, sales, personal development, and organizational development. Jody has co-authored more than 30 training programs on supervision, management, leadership, and inter-generational leadership.

Jody has worked for the State of Texas modifying the behaviors of former convicts, designed leadership programs for the Boy Scouts of America, and successfully built and sold 3 companies. Jody is a keynote speaker, author, and trainer… His fun and witty style of interaction has landed him the title of Chief Edu-Tainer!

Check out Jody's Website @:

www.JodyHolland.com

Book A Speaker @:

www.OurNextSpeaker.com

Made in the USA
San Bernardino, CA
20 June 2016